My Poetic Soul

J.S. Andersen

J.S. ANDERSEN

Denim Blues
Denim Blues
Nampa, ID 83686

Formatting: Denim Blues
Pictures: Front and back cover, Canva.com
                   Internal, Free clip art

ISBN-13: 978-0-578-51144-3
ISBN-10: 0-578-51144-4

J.S. ANDERSEN

What is Poetry?

I never liked poetry,
never understood the words they used
and what they were trying to say.
it made little sense.

But here I am now
writing my own thoughts down
from my deep inner soul for
someone else to read and wonder
what the hell is she trying to say?

????

J.S. ANDERSEN

Dark and Lost

J.S. ANDERSEN

You Are Okay

Shivering, frantic, a little frightened.
my mind has a mind of its own,
of self-control.

I need comfort and strength
but can't find it.
I need relief I need support.
is there anything out there?

Breathe, breathe, slowly let it out.
it's okay, it's okay.
everything's going to be all right.
you're okay, you're okay.

J.S. ANDERSEN

Dwindling

I ask for prayer and comfort
as my body is losing its defeat
it's deteriorating

Weeks have gone by
my strength has weakened.
my inner toughness is
dwindling to nothing.

I'm tired of feeling this way
I like nothing getting in my way.
and the bed is getting boring
laying in it day after day after day.

J.S. ANDERSEN

Empty

Having any connection would blow
any trust we had on each other-
would we cheat if we were a couple?
sometimes it is greener on the
other side of the fence.

I have never been hurt so bad
when someone walked out
of my life for good and tore a bigger
peace of love from my heart
then I thought I ever had.

I hurt badly; I'm crying because
I just lost my only close friend
some of it was my fault
but you helped feed it.

I feel empty, lost, and hurt.
there are more feelings for
you then I thought I had.
it will probably be better
in the long run.

Good Bye.

J.S. ANDERSEN

Going too Far

Feelings can overcome
common sense.
vulnerable and physical actions
are done with no thought
beforehand.

Is losing something you care about
more hurtful then pushing yourself
away to give space
and to help you face reality?

What you can't have,
you can't have. But stop before
you ruin a friendship for good.

J.S. ANDERSEN

Is Waiting Worth It?

Empty, lost, pain, and hurt.
I'm weak, sore, and tired of caring.
tired of trying, tired of wanting,
and tired of waiting.

Waiting for care, comfort, support,
waiting for the loving, understanding,
to ease my pain.

Waiting for a helping hand
to physically take my pain away,
and lead me out of my misery.

Help me break my mental
prison wall and walk me
to a peaceful semblance.

J.S. ANDERSEN

Insecurity

I'm very insecure.
I look down on myself
because I feel like a nobody.

Vulnerability became my weakness,
and will do things easy to please,
to get any pat on my back
for a feeling of accomplishment.

I want to be noticed for
someone that can do something
great and wonderful.
I want people to think that
I am worth something
and that I stand out.

J.S. ANDERSEN

Hurtful Love

I can read between the lines
of your words and body language.
I can sense the look of your eyes
that is thick of ice.
my arms are getting tired
trying to crack into
with an ice pick.

I'm your friend, not a dark
demon trying to ruin your life.
give me a chance to make your
life happier so I don't continue
to feel your pain and agony.

J.S. ANDERSEN

J.S. ANDERSEN

Gray and Hope

J.S. ANDERSEN

Backing Off

The thought of you tightens
my stomach in pain-the hoping
for your eyes looking at me
to feel what is running in your mind.
I know when you think of me.
I can feel your presence.

The wanting if stronger than you want
and you have a hard time controlling
your deep care for me
because there is more to it then you
want and can control.

I'll let go to lighten your load
to make your life happier and at peace.
I have a daringness part of me that
likes to play a little bit with fire.
this time I was a little too much daring
and stepped past my comfort and control.

J.S. ANDERSEN

I haven't burnt past healing yet,
and it probably won't happen,
but I'm sure I'll have some
permanent burnt marks.
The feeling's so strong,
but it doesn't feel bad
even though it should be.

J.S. ANDERSEN

Emotions Up or Down

Wither it's down
or wither it's up,
I'm tired of trying
to play those games,
I can't play those
games no more.
I'm out of here.
I'm out of here.

One minute we talk.
one minute we laugh.
one minute we share feelings,
then you shut the door in my face.
I don't hear from you on countless times.

J.S. ANDERSEN

Time of comfort

There's a time of comfort
being in a clear zone
no thoughts of bad feelings or good
a time to slumber and relax.

Your eyes are closed as you lay
snuggling on top of your bed.
drifting a little deeper,
your subconscious released thoughts
you never knew you had or
where they came from.

They can be pleasant and a little risky.
and you wonder if
it could ever come true
Is it a personal vision of
a future chance with a change?
or is it a wish or a want
or only a thought?

I guess it's time to take a
step and see what
will happen if it's
meant to be.

J.S. ANDERSEN

Ride of a Life Time

The feelings are like a roller coaster
either it's up really high at times
with past excitement and a little fear.

And other times it's low-
past low for a feeling not stopping.
you want out and never want to face Reality.

At times it is flat with no thrill
or excitement-a quick turn here
a quick turn there-but nothing tragic
to add any feelings at all.

Wish it was more of a stable ride
with only a few turns and short
climbs and downs.

Guess it's time to reconstruct
the roller coaster (ride) with
a different design.

J.S. ANDERSEN

Feelings

Thoughts can bring
scary feeling,
good feelings,
but uncontrollable
scary feelings
you didn't even know
you had those feelings,
and wish you didn't
cross that thin rail
because all the
feelings poured out.
You can't step back
and take those
feelings away, but
can use it in a
caring friendly way.

J.S. ANDERSEN

Sunny and Bright

J.S. ANDERSEN

One Day at a Time

You try walking fast,
to get things done,
but soon you're tuckered out
and fall behind.
Do your own stride
and have a smile.
At the end of the day
what isn't accomplished
can be done the next day.

```
O N E
  D A Y
A T   A
T I M E
```

J.S. ANDERSEN

How I feel

I thirst for your lips
I hunger for your touch
I melt for your body
Touch me, hold me, and caress me
let my mind get carried away.
I feel dizzy
I feel light
I feel ecstatic
I feel delighted
I feel moldable
I feel at ease.

J.S. ANDERSEN

Shinning Stars

The stars are brightly blinking
the leaves are dancing
in the cool breeze.
It's tingling and refreshing my skin.

Your eyes glitter
in the moon rays.
No words are required
to express how you feel.
Nor is the touch of your hand needed.

The passion is strong
like a magnet, it brings a smile to my face.
I lean on your strong chest for
support as my legs weaken.

I feel the warmth of
your body and the
comfort pouring in.

The magic is there
and will never fade
like the sunset at
the end of the day.

J.S. ANDERSEN

A Piece of my Heart

I've let a piece of me go that
hurts more than I thought would.
A change in life, like
People and emotions,
Are sometimes some good and bad.

I let go of a really close friend-
but it's better for me in the
long run to do so.
When I looked at the person's picture
It brought back feelings
I shouldn't even think about.

J.S. ANDERSEN

Feelings Never Die

The connection is so strong
I can feel his presence
feel his hand on my face
and my head on his shoulder.

His arm wrapped around me
holding me firmly and gave me comfort.
The thought has crossed my mind
often that he would be the
one to call my name in the hereafter
so we can be together forever.

He can feel it too.
Maybe it's just the med's I'm on
that makes me feel this way?
No- the feeling happened before.

J.S. ANDERSEN

Passion

To look into your eyes
I can't hold a stare
because passion is there.

The want of your hands
on my face and your
lips on mine are past
the unbearable.

The feeling will stay
deep in my heart
because you are
out of my reach.

J.S. ANDERSEN

Cleansing of the Mind

The world is beautiful
If you open your eyes and see.
The thought of being an eagle
Soaring in the air,
Seeing the clear beauty
Is a want and would be
Neat to have.

The rustle of leaves
sounding in a gentle breeze,
is soothing and relaxing.
Nature is safety, laying
out in the open with no
people talking, no phone ringing,
T.V. blasting, horns honking,
the smell of pollution.

It's a burden lifted off me
to clear my mind
of worldly things.

J.S. ANDERSEN

You Are Here

I never feel alone,
even when I'm standing
in an empty place.

I feel someone staring at me.
I look around and see no one.
Your closeness is felt like your
looking over me and you're close
within arm's reach.

I feel safe, protected, and not lonely.
Though I can't see you,
I know I'm in your mind,
and in your thoughts.
The feelings are strong
because I can feel it, too.

J.S. ANDERSEN

Don't Give-up

You want things
want to do things
things need to be accomplished.
So many steps
so many steps to take
not sure which way to go.

Too many choices,
too many closed doors.
Close your eyes
close your eyes and step.

Not what you want?
No big deal.
You learned from that step and
the next step will be better.

Don't' give-up on
taking blind steps.
You won't know the
outcome unless you do.

J.S. ANDERSEN

Connection

The feeling of connection is strong.
We can feel it in eye contact.
We can't hold a stare for the magnetic force
urging us to touch, to hold each other
and exchange passion from within.

Walking on a path by the river at dusk, talking,
he stops by a tree, and as his hands touch your
face,
he slowly turns your body until your back is
leaning against the tree trunk.

The sound of the river and crickets fade away
when his tender lips touch yours, your head
feels dizzy, and your knees grow weak.

You put your hands on his chest
and slowly move them up and around his neck.
The feel of his tongue tickling your lips
is making you drop your guard,

J.S. ANDERSEN

For you are tingling in many places,
your strength weakens.
The kiss slows to an end
and gently he runs his finger down
your nose and your lips.

His hand grabs yours and
you walk down the path,
fading into the darkness.
Right down in my heart
you'll always be.

J.S. ANDERSEN

Changes

Something has changed in my life
since the move across the country.
The hassle and bustle are
still the same, but an
inner old self I
thought was forever gone,
is resurfacing
with a full bang.

It comes in spurts
at unknown times, but when
it does with pen in hand,
I write what flows through my brains.

Later in time, I look back
and read what I wrote,
and am quite amassed at what I read
was actually from me.

J.S. ANDERSEN

This book covers the dark, gray, and light of my life. We all think differently and I'm sure you have felt the same as I have in one way or another.

I hope we all can see light before the end of the tunnel.

J.S. ANDERSEN

Here are a few extra pages for you to write
down your own Poetic Soul

_____

_____

_____

_____

_____

_____

_____

_____

_____

_____

_____

_____

_____

_____

_____

_____

_____

_____

_____

_____

_____

_____

_____

_____

J.S. ANDERSEN

_____
_____
_____
_____
_____
_____
_____
_____
_____
_____
_____
_____
_____
_____
_____
_____
_____
_____
_____
_____
_____
_____

www.ingramcontent.com/pod-product-compliance
Lightning Source LLC
Chambersburg PA
CBHW060648030426
42337CB00018B/3510